COOL CATS

Abyssinians

by Rebecca Felix

BLASTOFF! READERS 2

BELLWETHER MEDIA • MINNEAPOLIS, MN

Note to Librarians, Teachers, and Parents:

Blastoff! Readers are carefully developed by literacy experts and combine standards-based content with developmentally appropriate text.

Level 1 provides the most support through repetition of high-frequency words, light text, predictable sentence patterns, and strong visual support.

Level 2 offers early readers a bit more challenge through varied simple sentences, increased text load, and less repetition of high-frequency words.

Level 3 advances early-fluent readers toward fluency through increased text and concept load, less reliance on visuals, longer sentences, and more literary language.

Level 4 builds reading stamina by providing more text per page, increased use of punctuation, greater variation in sentence patterns, and increasingly challenging vocabulary.

Level 5 encourages children to move from "learning to read" to "reading to learn" by providing even more text, varied writing styles, and less familiar topics.

Whichever book is right for your reader, Blastoff! Readers are the perfect books to build confidence and encourage a love of reading that will last a lifetime!

This edition first published in 2016 by Bellwether Media, Inc.

No part of this publication may be reproduced in whole or in part without written permission of the publisher. For information regarding permission, write to Bellwether Media, Inc., Attention: Permissions Department, 5357 Penn Avenue South, Minneapolis, MN 55419.

Library of Congress Cataloging-in-Publication Data

Felix, Rebecca, 1984- author.
  Abyssinians / by Rebecca Felix.
    pages cm. – (Blastoff! Readers. Cool Cats)
  Summary: "Relevant images match informative text in this introduction to Abyssinian cats. Intended for students in kindergarten through third grade"– Provided by publisher.
  Audience: Ages 5-8
  Audience: K to grade 3
  Includes bibliographical references and index.
  ISBN 978-1-62617-229-6 (hardcover: alk. paper)
  1. Abyssinian cat–Juvenile literature. 2. Cats–Juvenile literature. I. Title.
  SF449.A28F45 2016
  636.8′26–dc23
                        2015001380

Printed in the United States of America, North Mankato, MN.

Table of
Contents

What Are Abyssinians?

Abyssinians are a lively cat **breed**.

They are active and **curious**.

These cats are short-haired.
Their fur has special coloring.

Abyssinians are also known for their large, pointed ears.

No one is sure about Abyssinians' original home. Some people think it was Egypt. These cats look like those in old Egyptian art.

Some studies show Abyssinians might be from Southeast Asia.

Southeast Asia

Egypt

N
W E
S

Abyssinians were **bred** in England in the 1800s.

They were brought to North America in the 1900s. They are a popular pet in the United States today.

Huge Ears and Ticked Hairs

Abyssinian ears are large and set far apart. They make the cats look **alert**.

Their eyes are also big. They are almond-shaped and usually green or gold.

Abyssinians have **ticked** fur. Each hair has many colors. The lightest color is close to the body.

Abyssinian Coats

ruddy

red

blue

fawn

The four common **coat** colors are called **ruddy**, red, blue, and **fawn**.

Abyssinians have medium-sized bodies. They are long and **lean**. Their tails are long, too.

Abyssinian Profile

— large, pointed ears

— large, almond-shaped eyes

— ticked fur

— long, lean body

Weight: 6 to 12 pounds (3 to 6 kilograms)

Life Span: 12 to 15 years

Active and Affectionate

Abyssinians like to play and climb up high.

They also love exploring. Some can open cupboards and doors! This breed is thought to be very smart.

Abyssinians do not usually like
to be picked up or held. But they
are **affectionate**.

They often follow
their owners around
the house!

Glossary

affectionate—loving

alert—paying attention to what is around

bred—purposely mated two cats to make kittens with certain qualities

breed—a type of cat

coat—the hair or fur covering an animal

curious—interested or excited to learn or know about something

fawn—a light tan and white color

lean—thin

ruddy—a brownish red color

ticked—having many lines of colors

To Learn More

AT THE LIBRARY

Bluemel Oldfield, Dawn. *Abyssinians: Egyptian Royalty?* New York, N.Y.: Bearport Pub., 2011.

Micco, Trudy. *Discover Abyssinian Cats.* Berkeley Heights, N.J.: Enslow Publishers, 2012.

Sexton, Colleen. *The Life Cycle of a Cat.* Minneapolis, Minn.: Bellwether Media, 2011.

ON THE WEB

Learning more about Abyssinians is as easy as 1, 2, 3.

1. Go to www.factsurfer.com.

2. Enter "Abyssinians" into the search box.

3. Click the "Surf" button and you will see a list of related web sites.

With factsurfer.com, finding more information is just a click away.

Index

The images in this book are reproduced through the courtesy of: Kalmatsuy, front cover, pp. 9, 17; nelik, p. 4; Juniors Bildarchiv/ Glow Images/ Superstock/ Age Fotostock, pp. 5, 6, 18; Nataliya Kuznetsova, p. 7; Werner Forman Archive/ Glow Images, p. 8; Superstock/ Glow Images, p. 10; Yulia Vybornyh, pp. 11, 20; Roxana Bashyrova, p. 12; Dr. Margorius, p. 13; Alan Robinson/ Kimball Stock, pp. 14-15; dien, p. 15 (top left); Linn Currie, p. 15 (top right); Gerard Lacz Images / Superstock, p. 15 (bottom left); Erich Schmidt/ Glow Images, p. 15 (bottom right); Denys Dolnikov, p. 16; kretsu, p. 19; Kirill Vorobyev, p. 21.